Granada
Travel Guide

Quick Trips Series

No part of this publication may be reproduced, stored in a retrieval system, or transmitted, in any form or by any means without the prior written permission of the publisher, nor be otherwise circulated in any form of binding or cover other than that in which it is published and without similar condition being imposed on the subsequent purchaser. If there are any errors or omissions in copyright acknowledgements the publisher will be pleased to insert the appropriate acknowledgement in any subsequent printing of this publication. Although we have taken all reasonable care in researching this book we make no warranty about the accuracy or completeness of its content and disclaim all liability arising from its use.

Copyright © 2016, Astute Press
All Rights Reserved.

Table of Contents

GRANADA — 5
- 🌎 CUSTOMS & CULTURE 7
- 🌎 GEOGRAPHY 9
- 🌎 WEATHER & BEST TIME TO VISIT 11

SIGHTS & ACTIVITIES: WHAT TO SEE & DO — 14
- 🌎 THE ALHAMBRA 14
  - Alcazaba 16
  - Generalife 16
  - Palace of Charles V 18
- 🌎 CATHEDRAL OF GRANADA 19
- 🌎 THE ROYAL CHAPEL 20
- 🌎 MONASTERY OF SAN JERÓNIMO DE GRANADA 21
- 🌎 MONASTERY OF CARTUJA 22
- 🌎 PALACE OF LA MADRAZA 22
- 🌎 ALBAYZIN 23
- 🌎 CORRAL DEL CARBON 26
- 🌎 SACROMONTE (GYPSY QUARTER) 27
  - Museo Cuevas del Sacromonte 29
- 🌎 REALEJO 30
- 🌎 SQUARES & PARKS 32
- 🌎 FAJALAUZA 35

BUDGET TIPS — 37

⊕ ACCOMMODATION 37
    Hotel Universal 37
    Hotel Posada del Toro 38
    El Granado 39
    Sidorme Granada Hotel 40
    El Abanico Sun Caves 41

⊕ PLACES TO EAT 42
    La Parrala Paella Bar 42
    Greens & Berries 43
    Los Diamantes 44
    La Bella y La Bestia 44
    Taberna Del Beso 45

⊕ SHOPPING 46
    Alcaiceria 46
    La Tiende de la Alhambra 47
    Taracea & Other Crafts 48
    Neptune Mall 50
    Festival Discos 50

KNOW BEFORE YOU GO   52

⊕ ENTRY REQUIREMENTS 52
⊕ HEALTH INSURANCE 52
⊕ TRAVELLING WITH PETS 53
⊕ AIRPORTS 54
⊕ AIRLINES 55
⊕ CURRENCY 56
⊕ BANKING & ATMS 56
⊕ CREDIT CARDS 56
⊕ TOURIST TAXES 57
⊕ RECLAIMING VAT 57
⊕ TIPPING POLICY 58

- **MOBILE PHONES** 59
- **DIALLING CODE** 60
- **EMERGENCY NUMBERS** 60
- **PUBLIC HOLIDAYS** 60
- **TIME ZONE** 61
- **DAYLIGHT SAVINGS TIME** 62
- **SCHOOL HOLIDAYS** 62
- **TRADING HOURS** 62
- **DRIVING LAWS** 63
- **DRINKING LAWS** 63
- **SMOKING LAWS** 64
- **ELECTRICITY** 64
- **FOOD & DRINK** 65

GRANADA TRAVEL GUIDE

Granada

In Granada, the Nazrids sought to create a paradise on earth and in the opulent splendour and beauty of the Alhambra, the wistful memory of that lost empire endures. Declared a UNESCO World Heritage site in 1984, the

GRANADA TRAVEL GUIDE

Alhambra draws two million visitors a year, making it one of Spain's most popular tourist attractions.

For holidaymakers, Granada combines a rich diversity of options. It lies within easy reach of the ski resorts of the Sierra Nevada mountains, but the sun-soaked beaches of Costa del Sol are equally accessible. This makes Granada the gateway to a rich variety of landscapes and activities.

There is more to Granada than meets the eye. With its tea shops and spice merchants, it still retains hints of its Moorish past, particularly within the picturesque streets and squares of the Albayzin. Equally hypnotic, is the fiery flamenco traditions of the Sacromonte gypsies. Oh, and did I mention the free food? The tapas bars of Granada religiously observe a tradition of serving complimentary snacks with each and every drink. Now that's what you call hospitality.

Granada is widely acknowledged to be one of the most beautiful cities in Spain. A well-known saying often seen on souvenirs, declares: *Give him alms, woman, for there is nothing as bad as being blind in Granada*, a quote sometimes attributed to the Mexican poet, Francisco de Icaza. When you come to the city of the Red Fortress, feast your eyes and feed your soul.

🌎 Customs & Culture

The city is known for a buoyant street life, and an added bonus is the tapas culture, still observed in many of Granada's watering holes. This involves the serving of

GRANADA TRAVEL GUIDE

generous complimentary snacks with each glass of wine of bar, meaning that it is easy to enjoy a filling lunch or supper, for the price of a few drinks.

The people of Granada tend to be late risers, but they make up for it, by partying to the early hours of the morning. Do not expect to dine before 8pm.

The region of Andalucía has always had a strong musical culture, even before flamenco became popular. While flamenco often touches on dramatic and emotion themes, older folk music expressive a cheerful and festive spirit. Contemporary music can take the form of a fusion of flamenco with rock, blues, salsa or rumba. Another regional music form is zarzuela, a blend of light opera with folk. If you are a musician yourself, it is a good place to

GRANADA TRAVEL GUIDE

look for a hand crafted guitar, as there are several guitar makers of renown in Granada. At any time, in a restaurant or bar, you may be surprised by an impromptu display of musicianship or dancing.

In general, Spain is quite monocultural. Over 90 percent of the population is white and subscribes to the Roman Catholic faith. While most Spaniards can be quite friendly, Granadinos have a reputation for being somewhat cantankerous. Despite the surface Spanish veneer, the city of Granada hides various pockets of more exotic flavor, such as the Moorish restaurants and teashops, and the Gypsy quarter.

There is a strong student presence in Granada. It is estimated that one in four residents are students. This

GRANADA TRAVEL GUIDE

means that, while the city has a vibrant night life, it is often quieter during the holiday periods. The bars around Pedro Alarcon attract a fairly young crowd, while the night scene around Calle Elvira is somewhat more mature and includes venues for jazz and flamenco.

The city hosts an international jazz festival in November. There is a long tradition of language and translation studies, probably dating back to the renowned Jewish translator YehubaIbnTibon. The author and playwright Federico Garcia Lorca was a native of Granada.

🌐 Geography

Granada can be found at the confluence of the Darro, Beiro and Genil rivers and to the south of the Sierra Nevada mountains. Spread across three hills, it is located

GRANADA TRAVEL GUIDE

about 70km from the coast, at an altitude of about 630m. The city of Granada is the capital of the province of the same name, which is located in the region of Andalucía.

Granada does not have an international airport, but is accessible by air, via Barcelona, Madrid and Malaga. It can also be reached by rail via Madrid, Barcelona and Valencia. A regular bus service connects Granada to Malaga, and also to Seville, Madrid and Cordoba. An inner city route runs along Gran Via, including a central stop near the Cathedral. Another option would be the brightly colored red and white Alhambra buses, that connect to various tourist sites. Bus tickets cost €1.20 per ride, but there are discounts for multiple use. The bus system uses audio-visual display boards and an SMS system to keep commuters updated on schedules.

GRANADA TRAVEL GUIDE

The Alhambra lies just to the south of Granada. It is surrounded by four neighbourhoods, each with its own culture and historical identity. Albayzin, the Moorish or Arabic quarter begins roughly where Calle Elvira connects with Plaza Nueva.

Streets are narrow, steep and cobbled, but there are several attractive little squares. Realejo was once the Jewish Quarter. From the Alhambra, it is accessible via the streets between the Carmenes and Puertadel Sol. The Old Quarter includes various religious structures, such as the Cathedral, located between Albayzin and the Alhambra. Along the hillside, you will find the cave homes of the Sacromonte, or Gypsy Quarter. To the south of the city lies Barrio de los Pajaritos.

GRANADA TRAVEL GUIDE

🌐 Weather & Best Time to Visit

Granada enjoys an abundance of sunshine year round. The climate is mild on average, seeing long, hot and dry summers and short, cool winters. Rain occurs during autumn and the early part of winter, with November generally being the wettest month. Spring and Autumn are the best times to visit Granada. Some people prefer winter, when hotel rates are at its cheapest, but it can get quite chilly.

In the months of high summer, day temperatures average around 33 degrees Celsius, but could go as high as 40 degrees Celsius. Night temperatures typically drop to around 17 degrees Celsius in July and August. Since it can get quite hot in the summer months, the culture is very much geared towards observing the siesta, when

GRANADA TRAVEL GUIDE

shops and restaurants close. In June and September, the day temperatures average between 28 and 29 degrees Celsius, while night temperatures stay around 14 degrees Celsius.

Even in October and May, day temperatures remain in the low to mid twenties, while night temperatures of around 10 degrees Celsius occur on average. April sees temperatures between 19 and 6 degrees Celsius.

In December, January and February, day temperatures between 12 and 14 degrees Celsius can be expected, while night temperatures may hover between 1 and 3 degrees Celsius. In the nearby Sierra Nevada Mountains, it can drop to -10 degrees Celsius in winter. In November and March, day temperatures between 16 and 17 degrees

GRANADA TRAVEL GUIDE

Celsius and night temperatures between 4 and 5 degrees Celsius can be experienced. Although snow is rare, light ground frosts can occur in the winter months.

GRANADA TRAVEL GUIDE

Sights & Activities: What to See & Do

🌏 The Alhambra

The Alhambra or the Red Fortress is one of the wonders of Moorish Spain. Located on a hill overlooking Granada, it resembles an entire walled city. There are three main sections.

GRANADA TRAVEL GUIDE

The Alcazaba was the fortified head quarters of the Alhambra's military wing. The second section includes various ornate palaces, including the Palace of the Lions, the Mexuar, which served as administrative and judicial center, Comares Palace and, a later addition, the Palace of Carlos V.

The Tower of Comares is at 45m, the highest of the Alhambra. The Palace of the Lions includes various architectural elements that are deeply symbolic. The twelve lion statues represent the twelve signs of the Zodiac, while the four rivers in the garden refer to paradise. The beautiful gardens of the third section or Generalife were created as a place of recreation.

GRANADA TRAVEL GUIDE

Mohammed I, the founder of the Nazrid dynasty, first conceived the fortified defences, built to strengthen the original castle, but some of the more elaborate structures can be attributed to Yusuf I and Mohammed V. Expect to spend at least three hours exploring the Alhambra. Admission for all three sections is €14.30.

Alcazaba

The defensive capabilities of the Alhambra were concentrated in the section known as the Alcazaba. This is one of the oldest parts of the complex and it may have been constructed over the remains of a Roman fortress.

The citadel includes four towers. The Torre de la Vela or watchtower, the Torre Quebrada or 'broken' tower and the Torre del Homenaje were built by Mohammed I. Torre de la Pólvora or the gunpowder tower was added later. Plaza de Armas or Armoury Square served as soldiers' barracks. Facilities for the soldiers, such as steam baths, food silos and an arsenal were also constructed. There were dungeons below the Alcazaba and water reserves in the basement.

Generalife

Located on Cerro del Sol or the Hill of the Sun, Generalife provides an excellent vantage point from which to observe the valleys of the Genil and Darro river. It was created during the 13th century, but during the early 14th century, King Abu l-Walid Isma'il redecorated the complex.

For the Nazrid rulers of Granada, it offered a place of leisure and respite and it is easy to see why, even today.

GRANADA TRAVEL GUIDE

In summer, fragrant flowers are abloom and the garden is refreshed by various decorative fountains and water features. The Patio of the Irrigation Ditch is the most pivotal part of the complex. A channel system drove water from the Alhambra, dividing it into several jets that end in stone basins. The one side is resplendid with plants such as rose and myrtle bushes, and orange and cypress trees. At the other end of the patio, there is a wall with eighteen ogival arches, which dates back 1670. At the northern and southern end, two pavilions enclosed the patio.

After Moorish rule ended, some Christian structures, such as the West Gallery were added. Admission is €7 for the Generalife. A combo ticket to the Generalife and the Alhambra will cost €13.

Palace of Charles V

Charles V, grandson of Ferdinand and Isabelle inherited the throne of Spain and built a palace within the Alhambra's fortified walls. The gesture was meant to symbolize the triumph of Christianity over Islam.

The palace was first conceived in 1526 and construction began around 1533, according to the original designs of Pedro Machuca. By 1550, the facade was completed. Around this time, Pedro died and his son, Luis created a circular courtyard. The Moorish rebellion in 1568 put a stop to the construction and during the 1600s, work was abandoned.

Around 1923, Leopoldo Torres Balbas came up with plans to complete the palace at last. Its design is based on classical Roman styles. The building now houses the exhibitions of the Fine Arts Museum on the top floor and the Alhambra Museum, on the ground floor. The courtyard is sometimes used for concerts. Admission is free.

🌐 Cathedral of Granada

Gran Via de Colon 5, 18001 Granada

Tel: +34 (0) 95 822 2959

The cathedral of Granada is a good example of the shift from Gothic to Renaissance that was evident in Spain during the 16th century. The building occupies the site of a former mosque and its foundations, laid by the architect Enrique Egas, still show clear Gothic influences.

Construction began under Diego de Siloé, but since the cathedral took over 180 years to complete, various subsequent architects, such as Juan de Maena, Juan de Orea, Ambrosio de Vico, Gaspar de la Peña and Alonso Cano left their mark on the project. Some of the conceived features never translated to reality, but the building can still be regarded as an impressive celebration of ecclesiastic architecture. Some notable elements are the beautiful dome and ceiling stained glass work, various sculptures , including busts of Adam and Eve by Alonso Cano and the Triumph Arch. Admission is €4.

🌐 The Royal Chapel

Capilla Real, Gran Via de Colon 5, 18001 Granada

Tel.:+34 (0)95 822 7848

http://www.capillarealgranada.com/

GRANADA TRAVEL GUIDE

The Royal Chapel was built between 1505 and 1527 to house the remains of Ferdinand and Isabella, the driving force behind the Reconquesta, at the location of their final victory. The style is Gothic and it was dedicated to St John the Baptist and St John the Evangelist. The mausoleum contains the remains of Isabella I, Ferdinand II, their daughter Queen Juana of Castille, their son-in-law, Phillip I and Miguel da Paz, prince of Asturias, Portugal and Girona, who died in Granada before his second birthday.

Initially Charles V moved several other royal graves to the site, but Phillip II removed most of these to a newly constructed Escorial. The Royal Chapel is connected to the Cathedral, but with its own integrity of design. Some of its ornamental features include gargoyles, decorative art incorporating the Royal Initials and heraldic emblems as well as a statue of the Virgin Mary. Admission is €3.50.

🌐 Monastery of San Jerónimo de Granada

Calle Rector LópezArgueta, 9, 18001 Granada, Spain

Tel: +34 958 27 93 37

The Monastery of San Jerónimo de Granada was built in 1504, to house an order founded outside the city during the Siege of Granada. The sacristy is in Spanish Baroque style and the altar is by Gil de Siloe. It is open to the public and admission is €3.50.

GRANADA TRAVEL GUIDE

🌐 Monastery of Cartuja

Paseo de Cartuja, Granada

Tel: +34 958 161 932

The Monastery of Cartuja can be regarded as a great example of Baroque architecture. It includes a number of sculptures and paintings, including works by Juan Sánchez Cotán, that depict episodes from the history of the Carthusian order, as well as the Last Supper and Passion of Christ. Admission is €3.50.

🌐 Palace of La Madraza

Plaza de Isabel la Catolica, Granada

Tel: +34 (0)95 822 5990

Built in the 14th century, the Madraza was the first

GRANADA TRAVEL GUIDE

university of Granada. It was created under the auspices of the Nazarite king, Yusuf I and inaugurated in 1349. Some of the curriculum included theology, law, medicine and mathematics. It continued for a brief period after the Reconquesta as an educational facility, but after 1499, policies of tolerance gave way to forced conversions. The university's library was emptied and its contents burnt on the Plaza la Bib-Rambla, under the supervision of Cardinal Cisneros. For a time it was used as a chapter house, but eventually it fell into decay.

An 18th century restoration project added a Baroque staircase and balconies, but many of the original elements were lost or altered. In the oratory, soon of the Moorish decoration is still visible. Today, the Madraza palace houses various departments of the University of Granada. It is open to the public and admission is free.

🌐 Albayzin

Albayzin lies uphill and north of Plaza Nueva. The narrow streets and whitewashed historical buildings still retain tantalizing hints of the city's Moorish past.

Here you can expect to find Arabic restaurants, tea shops and curiosities from North Africa. A good spot to soak up some of the atmosphere, is As-Sirat on Placeta de la Charca, an authentic Arab tea shop that also plays Arabian music.

Another charming aspect of the Albayzin, would be its many 'carmens', the secluded gardens that were

GRANADA TRAVEL GUIDE

incorporated into the layout. One particularly beautiful example is the Carmen de los Mártires, which can be found close to Museo Manuel de Falla. It includes citrus and palm trees, fountains and even an artificial island.

A great location to get an overview of Granada, is Mirador de San Nicolas, one of the highest points of Albayzin. From this vantage point, you can see the Alhambra, the city Granada and the Sierra Nevada mountains. It can get quite crowded, especially in summer, but some of the nearby restaurants also offer spectacular views. You can simply stroll up the cobbled streets, from Plaza Nueva or Calle Elvira, but the number 31 bus from Gran Via should get you most of the way there.

GRANADA TRAVEL GUIDE

Just off Plaza San Nicolas, you will find the Mosque of Granada, a relatively new addition to the city, which nevertheless recalls the glorious architecture of the past and includes a fragrant garden. Admission is free. From Plaza Largo, off Calledel Agua del Albaicin, you can reach Placeta de las Minas, which adjoins a remaining section of one of the neighborhood's defensive walls.

A scenic walk of the Albayzin leads along Carrera delDarro, which parallels the Darro river from Plaza Nueva. At 31 Carrera delDarro, you could explore Hamman El Banuelo, one of the best-preserved Arabian bath houses in Spain. At the end of Carrera delDarro, you will reach Plaza de los Tristes, where several restaurants are clustered together. Here, too, you can enjoy good views of the Alhambra.

GRANADA TRAVEL GUIDE

🌏 Corraldel Carbon

Corral del Carbon, (Behind the City Hall)

18009 Granada

Tel: +34 958-225-990

One of the oldest monuments to Moorish rule is the Corral del Carbon, which was built by Yusuf I in the 14th century. In its heyday, it served as coal chamber, warehouse and inn for merchants. Charcoal was sold on its patio. The upper floors were used for human accommodation, while the lower floors served as stables, or storage space.

The facade features a horseshoe arch and includes epigraphic motifs as well as plasterwork resembling stalactites. The courtyard included galleries and craft rooms, as well as a central well. During the 16th century, it was adapted to become a stage. Today, it is used as location for summertime flamenco festivals and also houses the tourist office and a bookshop. Admission is free.

🌍 Sacromonte (Gypsy Quarter)

One of the most fascinating communities of Granada live in a network of caves above the Albayzin. The first Gypsies arrived in Spain during the 15th century and they acquired a reputation as good craftsmen and skilled animal herders.

There are various legends about their dugout homes. One suggests that the gypsies took to the hills during the 16th century, fearing persecution from the Christian Catholic rulers. Another alleges that fleeing Arab noblemen buried

GRANADA TRAVEL GUIDE

some of their treasures in Granada, in the hope that they would one day be able to return.

The African slaves they left behind, dug out the hillside caves in the hope of finding their masters' gold. Around 1950, there were over 3,600 cave dwellings, but floods have reduced the numbers. Sacromonte is the birthplace of zambra, a style of flamenco that combines song and dance, and is a little more Oriental in character. There is one main street, Camino delSacromonte, which is lined with various bars and restaurants, as well as flamenco venues.

Founded more than fifty years ago, María La Canastera's Zambra is a well-established celebration of the art of one of Granada's best-known flamenco dancers. It is still owned by her descendants, who keep the old traditions alive. There is also a small museum, which displays memorabilia. María La Canastera's Zambra is located at 89 Camino del Sacromonte and a shuttle service is available for visitors.

Ventadel Gallo is a landmark, as this is the highest point in the Sacromonte that you can reach by taxi. Here, you can dine and enjoy a flamenco show. Through the management at Venta del Gallo, you can also book a tour of Sacromonte or Albaycin. Located at 5 Barranco Los Negros 5, Venta del Gallo charges €22 for a flamenco show and €52 for a meal and show. Zambra Cuevadel Rocio provides an intimate experience of the dance, as the performers may dance right in front of you, rather than on a stage. Zambra Cuevadel Rocia can be found at 70 Camino del Sacromonte.

Museo Cuevas del Sacromonte

Barranco de los Negros; Sacromonte

Tel. +34 (0) 958-215-120

http://www.sacromontegranada.com/

Museo Cuevas del Sacromonte provides a fascinating glimpse into the colorful life and culture of Granada's Gypsy Quarter. The exhibition stretches across several of the caves and showcases some of the Gypsy crafts such as basket weaving, fabric weaving, metalwork and pottery. It offers insight into the utilities and possibilities of this unique environment.

GRANADA TRAVEL GUIDE

From time to time, visitors can view live demonstrations of various crafts. There are also other exhibits focused around the flora and fauna of the region, its agriculture and the unique geographical properties of Granada. The museum hosts a cultural programme that includes plays and other performing arts. Admission is €5.

🌎 Realejo

Now a vibrant and densely populated neighborhood, Realejo was once named Garnata al-Yahud or 'Granada of the Jews'. It is believed that the first Jews settled in the region of Granada as far back as 70 or 135 AD, but historical record first refers to their presence around 300 AD. Under Muslim rule, a spirit of tolerance existed towards the Jews, and they prospered through involvement in the silk and cotton trade. There were periodic tensions, such as a massacre in 1066.

Calle Pavaneras was the street of Jewish artisans such as cobblers and leather tanners. It is believed that a synagogue may have stood at the intersection of Calle San Matias and Calle Pavaneras. After the Reconquesta, Jews were expelled from the city. It is estimated that the Jewish population had numbered around 50,000 at the time. Much is this quarter's history is now obliterated or hidden, but occasionally, you may still glimpse a forgotten David's Star above a doorway.

An important feature is Campo de Principe, built on the site of a former Muslim cemetery. Laid out in 1497, this square was meant to commemorate the wedding of

GRANADA TRAVEL GUIDE

Prince Juan. It includes a statue, Christo de los Faveros, which was added in 1640, and was believed to be responsible for the inhabitants of Barrio Realejo escaping the devastation of the Bubonic plague. Today, the monument still draws crowds of devotees on Holy Friday.

Another location worth a visit is Casa de Los Tiros in Calle Pavaneras, once owned by the Marquis of Campotejar, but now a museum dedicated to documenting the history of Granada. Casa de la Juderia at 37 Calle Rodrigo del Campo includes a layout and some clues to the neighborhood's Jewish roots. Along CalleColcha, you might see the statue of Yehuba Ibn Tibon, a Jewish doctor, poet and translator of note, who lived in the 12th century. Other buildings of note include the Palace of los Condes de Gabia, the Church of San

GRANADA TRAVEL GUIDE

Cecilio, the Church of Santo Domingo, the Imperial Church of St Matthias, the House of Gran Capitan and Antigua Capitania, the Convent of the Mercedarias.

If you love informal art, there is another reason to add El Realejo to your itinerary. Many of the walls feature 'works' by the graffiti artist El Nino de las Pinturas, a native of the Realejo.

🌍 Squares & Parks

Although Plaza Nueva means "new square", it is in reality one of the oldest squares in Granada. Built over the river Darro and later expanded to reach Plaza of Santa Ana, it was once the site of bullfights, games, tournaments and even executions. The square is flanked by the Royal Chancellery, which dates back to 1530 and the Iglesia de

GRANADA TRAVEL GUIDE

San Gil y Santa Ana, which replaced the Almanzora mosque. Both buildings were designed by Diego de Siloé. A more recent addition is the Fountain of the Bull, installed in 1941. There are many nearby shops, bars and restaurants and it is close to the vibrant Calle Elvira and the enigmatic Albayzin.

The main feature of Plaza de Isabel la Católica is a statue depicting Queen Isabella approving the petition of Christopher Columbus, granting him ships and supplies for his voyages to the New World. It is located off Gran Vía de Colón and Calle Reyes Catílicos.

Bib Rambla has at various times been the setting of tournaments, festivals, bullfights, horse fairs and a vegetable market. It was also here that close to a million

GRANADA TRAVEL GUIDE

books from the library of the Palace of the Madraza were destroyed. At the center of the gate, is the Gigantones Fountain.

Carmen de los Mártires is located near the Alhambra and includes a memorial to the Christian martyrs who had been held captive by the Moors. Many of these worked as forced laborers on the palaces of Granada and died during the siege for the city. The site had at one time included a convent, but this was destroyed during the 1800s. Today, the garden is a blend of English and French landscaping. It includes numerous fountains, statues, grottoes, a tower and a wooden bridge. There are also ducks, black swans and peafowl in the garden and visitors can enjoy great views of the city and the Sierra

GRANADA TRAVEL GUIDE

Nevada mountains. Carmen de los Mártires is off Paseo de los Mártires

Triunfo Gardens was originally envisaged by Mayor D. Manuel Gadea on the site of a former Arab cemetery. With the encroachment of urban development and the construction of Gran Via de Colon, it moved to the location of the old bullfighting ring at Plaza de Toros. Its most striking features are the statue of Triunfo de la Virgen or "Triumph of the Virgin Mary" and a 75m long fountain that includes colored lights. There is a monument to San Juan de Dios and a second fountain in the lower part of Triunfo Gardens.

GRANADA TRAVEL GUIDE

🌍 Fajalauza

Carretera de Murcia, 15, Granada,

Tel: +34 958 28 13 91

http://www.fajalauza.com/

Fajalauza, a factory that produces tiles and ceramics has the reputation for being the longest running family business in Granada. Owned by the Morales family, it dates back all the way to the 17th century, when a Moorish businessman bowed to pressure to convert to Christianity. He took the name of Alonso de Morales.

Today, the factory still uses techniques and designs that have their roots in the city's Moorish past. Besides tiles, it produces jars, vases, bowls and plates - often with the typically Granadino colors of blue, green and purple and using symbols such as birds or pomegranates. Fajalauza

is open to the public for tours and also sales.

GRANADA TRAVEL GUIDE

GRANADA TRAVEL GUIDE

Budget Tips

🌐 Accommodation

Hotel Universal

C/ Recogidas 16,

18002 Granada (Realejo - San Matias)

Tel: +34 958 26 00 16

http://www.hoteluniversalgranada.com/

Hotel Universal is centrally located and has a TV lounge, a computer lounge and dining room. It has air-conditioning as well as central heating and offers wheelchair friendly facilities. Rooms include a mini-bar, bathroom facilities, hairdryer, television and direct telephone. Free Wi-Fi access is available throughout the hotel. Staff are described as friendly and helpful. Laundry services and private parking can be made available at an extra charge. Accommodation begins at €40 per night. A modest continental breakfast is served.

Hotel Posada del Toro

Calle Elvira, 25, 18010 Granada

Tel: +34 958 22 73 33

http://www.posadadeltoro.com/en/

The Hotel Posada del Toro is centrally located in lower Albaizin, at the heart of Granada and within easy walking distance of the Cathedral as well as several restaurants and tourist shops. It can get a little noisy, though and parking could be a problem for guests with their own transport. The interior features beautiful stained glass windows and there is an attractive central courtyard. Staff members are friendly and generally speak good English. Rooms include a flat screen TV, mini-bar, bathroom facilities and free wifi. Accommodation begins at €45 and includes a continental breakfast.

El Granado

CalleConde de Tendillas 7, 180 02 Granada (Centro - Sagrario)

Tel: +34 958 960 259

http://www.elgranado.com/

El Granado is centrally located, within walking distance of the main sights of Granado. Part of the building dates back to the Nazrid period, between the 13th and 15th century, but it has been refurbished and rooms are clean and spotlessly maintained.

GRANADA TRAVEL GUIDE

The hostel has a kitchen and a wifi zone, as well as a PC with unlimited internet access. Breakfast is free, but self-service. The reception staff are friendly and helpful. A variety of accommodation options are available. For the super cash-strapped backpacker, there is a shared dorm room, for €18 per night. Double rooms are available for €40 per night and apartments can be rented for between €60 and €105.

Sidorme Granada Hotel

C/ Luis Buñuel S/N À côté du C.C. Kinepolis 18197

Pulianas (Granada)

Tel: +34 95 818 52 57

http://www.sidorme.com/en/hotels/hotel-granada

GRANADA TRAVEL GUIDE

The Sidorme Granada Hotel is located about 8km from the city center, but offers excellent views of the nearby Sierra Nevada mountains. There is a bus stop nearby and a ticket to the city center will cost about €3. While some may consider this inconvenient, the hotel does offer excellent value for money. Rooms are equipped with central heating, flat screen TV, modern bathroom facilities and the choice of a hard or soft base bed. Free coffee, tea and hot chocolate are available at all hours. The hotel also has free high-speed wifi coverage. Accommodation begins at €20. An all-you-can-eat buffet breakfast is available at €3.

El Abanico Sun Caves

Verea de Enmedio 89, Granada

(from "ZambraMaría la Canastera", follow signs to Las

GRANADA TRAVEL GUIDE

Cuevas El Abanico)

Tel: +(34) 958 226199

http://www.cuevaselabanico.es/english.html

The Sacromonte Gypsy Quarter of Granada is unique. To truly immerse yourself in the experience, why not stay in one of Granada's cave dwellings. El Abanico Sun Caves offers holiday accommodation in one of five authentic Gypsy cave homes. Located near the Alhambra and Albayzin Arab Quarter, many of the city's sites are within easy walking distance. Since the caves are naturally cool, there is no air-conditioning. There is, however wifi coverage available. Each unit has a modest kitchen, bathroom facilities and a heater. Accommodation begins at €68 per day or €420 per week. Discounted rates are available for a longer stay. Towels, bedding and kitchen equipment are included, but housekeeping services will be charged separately.

🌏 Places to Eat

La Parrala Paella Bar

Calle Colcha, Granada

Tel: +34 (0)858995217

Paella is synonymous with Spain, and for a mouth-watering sample of seafood paella, you could not do much better than La Parrala Paella Bar. The service is friendly, the owners speak fluent English and you could enjoy a filling meal for around €10. You can also try the sangria and enjoy some of the complimentary tapas snacks such as spinach pancakes with blue cheese, toast with hummus and olives or tomato and mozzarella. La

Parralla Paella Bar is located just off Plaza Nuevo. While the seafood paella is a favorite, the restaurant also serves meat paella and vegetarian paella.

Greens & Berries

Plaza Nueva, 1, 18010 Granada (Realejo - San Matias)

Tel: +34(0)633895086

https://www.facebook.com/pages/Greens-Berries-Granada/106585002723404

For a refreshingly healthy alternative, try this restaurant which is located on Plaza Nueva.

Some of the meals include salads, muffins, brownies, sandwiches - with fillings such as chicken and a Mediterranean medley - as well as soups. Among the beverages, you can expect to enjoy lemonade, freshly squeezed fruit juices, smoothies or even a fruit based variant of sangria. Expect to pay between €2.50 and €8 per item.

Los Diamantes

Calle Navas, 26, Granada (Realejo - San Matias)

Tel: +34 (0)958 227 070

One of the good things about Granada is the abundant availability of free food at the price of a few drinks. At Los Diamantes, a notice states that the tapas is a gift, which you cannot choose or return. If you love seafood, you would not want to return anything, though. Among the tapas rounds that could make its way to your table, there is fried calamari, fried prawns, deep-fried aubergine chips, clams, mushrooms in garlic or paella. Los Diamantes is a local favorite, which means that your waiter may not speak the best English. The establishment is open between 12 and 2.30pm and again after 8pm.

La Bella y La Bestia

CalleCarcel Baja, 14, 18010 Granada (Realejo - San Matias)

Tel: +34 (0)958-229-812

http://www.bodegaslabellaylabestia.com/

Another tapas bar where you can snack on a variety of generously portioned tapas snacks for a few drinks is La Belle y La Bestia. The location is attractive and tranquil. Some of the snacks you can expect include vegetarian lasagne, roast potatoes, curry chicken sandwiches, a grilled bagel with Serrano ham, French fries, pasta salad or a local speciality, fried eggplant with honey. The tapas changes with each drink. You could opt for a plate of three tapas, sandwiches and French fries for €5. The establishment is one of a group of four eateries.

Taberna Del Beso

Cuesta De Las Arremangadas No. 6, Granada

Located in the Albayzin neighborhood, Taberna Del Beso offers both indoor and outdoor dining. The cuisine is Moroccan and includes dishes such as lamb pita, chicken kebabs, chicken curry, Harira soup, vegetable couscous and croquettes. Desserts consist of a selection of Moroccan pastries and beverages include various teas and sangria. Expect to pay around €21 for a meal for two. The free wifi is an added bonus. Another African style establishment to visit, is the tapas bar Om Khalsum on CalleJardines, which offers complimentary Moorish style tapas with each drink.

Shopping

Alcaiceria

Near Plaza Bib-Rambla

You can expect to be greeted by a colorful variety of rich ethnic patterns and shapes at the Alcaiceria, which still resembles an Arab souk. Shop here for hookah pipes, traditional Arab teas, shawls, dresses, lanterns, leather bags and many more. The name Alcaicería, dates back to the 6th century, when the Byzantine Emperor Justinian granted Arabs exclusive rights to trade in silk and was commonly used throughout Moorish Spain to signify a market or bazaar.

Today, the market is an excellent place to browse for souvenirs or craft items. Some of the goods on display include hand-painted ceramics, which is locally referred to as fajalauza, stained glass lanterns, also known as farolas and taracea - trinket boxes or chess-sets which feature wooden inlays. Visit the stalls nearest to Plaza Bib-Rambla, for Moroccan spices, silks and herbs. You can also buy ethnic clothing, Arabic craftwork and even a memento of your name in Arabic script.

La Tiende de la Alhambra

Calle Reyes Católicos 40 Granada

Tel. +34 (0)958 22 7846

Most people come to Granada to visit the Alhambra and want to go home with at least one souvenir depicting the city's most famous landmark. At La Tiende de la Alhambra, the main focus is on the Alhambra. Guidebooks to the Alhambra are available in various languages, but there are also books on history, architecture, photography, poetry and literature. In style, they range from children's art books to glossy coffee table tomes. The shop also stocks a variety of exclusive prints, post cards, photographs and illustrations. Other items include creative stationary and hand-painted fans.

Taracea & Other Crafts

Although the Christian rulers did their best to obliterate Granada's Muslim past, some reflections of a Moorish

GRANADA TRAVEL GUIDE

heritage linger in Granada. It is very much evident in a craft form that is particular to Granada. Taracea is the art of creating intricate, often geometrical patterns through marquetry, or the inlay of metal, bones, mother-of-pearl, tortoise shell or contrasting variants of wood. It is also practiced in Egypt and Syria.

There are a number of shops that specialize in taracea items. Artesania Gonzalez is the workshop of the Gonzalez family, who have practiced the craft for generations.

It is located at 2 Cuesta de Gomérez in Granada, just off Plaza Nueva. First opened in 1948, Artesania Beas trades from a shop at 20 Calle Santa Rosalía. It is a family business, and the workmanship of the products, which include small boxes, trays, coasters and chess sets is highly rated. At Laguna Taller de Taracea, you will be able to see the live demonstration of a skilled taracea artisan at work, and then buy his produce. The workshop is located at 30 Real de la Alhambra.

Artesania el Suspiro stocks a diversity of craft and gift items such as post cards, hand-made jewellery, Moroccan pottery and ceramics. There is a particularly large selection of ceramic items. The shop is located at 1 Plaza Santa Ana and staff members speak English. Ceramica Al Yarrar stocks reproductions of pottery of the Moorish period. The shop can be found at 6 Calle Joaquin Costa. Altrove specializes in African artefact and authentic African jewellery, with a slight emphasis on bead products. The shop is located at 2 CalleÁnimas.

Neptune Mall

Calle Arabial, 45, Granada

Tel: +34 958 52 22 45

http://www.webneptuno.com/

While Granada has many little shops full of character, it is not exactly overrun with modern shopping malls. The Neptune Mall has over a hundred shops, selling a variety of goods ranging from fashion, jewellery, toys, perfume and cosmetics.

Businesses worth a visit is the official Granada C.F. merchandize store, an art framing shop that also stocks vintage and modern prints and Game Stop, the world's largest video game outlet. The mall also has several restaurants and a movie theatre.

Festival Discos

Calle de San Sebastián, 10, 18001 Granada

Tel: +34 958 22 07 45

Granada has a rich musical heritage and at Festival Discos, you can buy music across a large selection of genres. The stock ranges from classical and opera to flamenco, modern Spanish, folk and rock. Expect to pay around €15 per CD on average.

GRANADA TRAVEL GUIDE

Know Before You Go

🌐 Entry Requirements

By virtue of the Schengen agreement, visitors from other countries in the European Union will not need a visa when visiting Spain. Additionally visitors from Switzerland, Norway, Lichtenstein, Iceland, Canada, the United Kingdom, Australia and the USA are also exempt. Independently travelling minors will need to carry written permission from their parents. If visiting from a country where you require a visa to enter Spain, you will also need to state the purpose of your visit and provide proof that you have financial means to support yourself for the duration of your stay. Unless you are an EU national, your passport should be valid for at least 3 months after the end of your stay.

🌐 Health Insurance

Citizens of other EU countries are covered for emergency health care in Spain. UK residents, as well as visitors from Switzerland are covered by the European Health Insurance Card (EHIC), which can be applied for free of charge. Visitors from non-Schengen countries will need to show proof of private health insurance that is valid for the duration of their stay in Spain, as part of their visa application.

🌐 Travelling with Pets

Spain participates in the Pet Travel Scheme (PETS) which allows UK residents to travel with their pets without requiring quarantine upon re-entry. Certain conditions will need to be met. The animal will have to be microchipped and up to date on rabies vaccinations. Additionally, you will need a PETS re-entry certificate issued by a UK vet, an Export Health Certificate (this is required by the Spanish authorities), an official Certificate of Treatment against dangerous parasites such as tapeworm and ticks and an official Declaration that your pet has not left the qualifying countries within this period. Pets from the USA or Canada may be brought in under the conditions of a non-commercial import. For this, your pet will also need to be microchipped (or marked with an identifying tattoo) and up to date on rabies vaccinations.

🌐 Airports

Adolfo Suárez Madrid–Barajas Airport (MAD) is the largest and busiest airport in Spain. It is located about 9km from the financial district of Madrid, the capital. The busiest route is the so-called "Puente Aéreo" or "air bridge", which connects Madrid with Barcelona. The second busiest airport in Spain is **Barcelona–El Prat Airport** (BCN), located about 14km southwest from the center of Barcelona. There are two terminals. The newer Terminal 1 handles the bulk of its traffic, while the older Terminal 2 is used by budget airlines such as EasyJet.

Palma de Mallorca Airport (PMI) is the third largest airport in Spain and one of its busiest in the summer time. It has the capacity of processing 25 million passengers annually. **Gran Canaria Airport** (LPA) handles around 10 million passengers annually and connects travellers with the Canary Islands. **Pablo Ruiz Picasso Malaga Airport** (AGP) provides access to the Costa del Sol. Other southern airports are **Seville Airport** (SVQ), **Jaen Federico Garcia Lorca Airport** (GRX) near Granada, **Jerez de la Frontera Airport**, which connects travellers to Costa del Luz and Cadiz and **Almeria Airport** (LEI).

🌐 Airlines

Iberia is the flag carrying national airline of Spain. Since a merger in 2010 with British Airways, it is part of the International Airlines Group (IAG). Iberia is in partnership with the regional carrier Air Nostrum and Iberia Express, which focusses on medium and short haul routes. Vueling is a low-cost Spanish airline with connections to over 100 destinations. In partnership with MTV, it also provides a seasonal connection to Ibiza. Volotea is a budget airline based in Barcelona, which mainly flies to European destinations. Air Europe, the third largest airline after Iberia and Vueling connects Europe to resorts in the Canaries and the Balearic Islands and also flies to North and South America. Swiftair flies mainly to destinations in Europe, North Africa and the Middle East.

Barcelona-El Prat Airport serves as a primary hub for Iberia Regional. It is also a hub for Vueling. Additionally it functions as a regional hub for Ryanair. Air Europe's primary hubs are at Palma de Mallorca Airport and Madrid Barajas Airport, but other bases are at Barcelona Airport and Tenerife South Airport. Air Nostrum is served by hubs at Barcelona Airport, Madrid Barajas Airport and Valencia Airport. Gran Canaria Airport is the hub for the regional airline, Binter Canarias.

🌐 Currency

Spain's currency is the Euro. It is issued in notes in denominations of €500, €200, €100, €50, €20, €10 and €5. Coins are issued in denominations of €2, €1, 50c, 20c, 10c, 5c, 2c and 1c.

🌐 Banking & ATMs

You should have no trouble making withdrawals in Spain if your ATM card is compatible with the MasterCard/Cirrus or Visa/Plus networks. If you want to save money, avoid using the dynamic currency conversion (DCC) system, which promises to charge you in your own currency for the Euros you withdraw. The fine print is that your rate will be less favorable. Whenever possible, opt to conduct your transaction in Euros instead. Do remember to advise your bank or credit card company of your travel plans before leaving.

🌐 Credit Cards

Visa and MasterCard will be accepted at most outlets that handle credit cards in Spain, but you may find that your American Express card is not as welcome at all establishments. While shops may still be able to accept transactions with older magnetic strip cards, you will need a PIN enabled card for transactions at automatic vendors such as ticket sellers. Do not be offended when asked to show proof of ID when paying by credit card. It is common practice in Spain and Spaniards are required by law to carry identification on them at all times.

🌐 Tourist Taxes

In the region of Catalonia, which includes Barcelona, a tourist tax of between €0.45 and €2.50 per night is levied for the first seven days of your stay. The amount depends on the standard of the establishment, but includes youth hostels, campgrounds, holiday apartments and cruise ships with a stay that exceeds 12 hours.

🌐 Reclaiming VAT

If you are not from the European Union, you can claim back VAT (or Value Added Tax) paid on your purchases in Spain. The VAT rate in Spain is 18 percent. VAT refunds are made on purchases of €90.15 and over from a single shop. Look for shops displaying Global Blue Tax Free Shopping signage. You will be required to fill in a form at the shop, which must then be stamped at the Customs office at the airport. Customs officers will want to inspect your purchases to make sure that they are sealed and unused. Once this is done, you will be able to claim your refund from the Refund Office at the airport. Alternately, you can mail the form to Global Blue once you get home for a refund on your credit card.

GRANADA TRAVEL GUIDE

🌍 Tipping policy

In general, Spain does not really have much of a tipping culture and the Spanish are not huge tippers themselves. When in a restaurant, check your bill to see whether a gratuity is already included. If not, the acceptable amount will depend on the size of the meal, the prestige of the restaurant and the time of day. For a quick coffee, you can simply round the amount off. For lunch in a modest establishment, opt for 5 percent or one euro per person. The recommended tip for dinner would be more generous, usually somewhere between 7 and 10 percent. This will depend on the type of establishment.

In hotels, if there is someone to help you with your luggage, a tip of 1 euro should be sufficient. At railway stations and airports, a tip is not really expected. Rounding off the amount of the fare to the nearest euro would be sufficient for a taxi driver. If you recruited a private driver, you may wish to tip that person at the end of your association with him.

🌍 Mobile Phones

Most EU countries, including Spain uses the GSM mobile service. This means that most UK phones and some US and Canadian phones and mobile devices will work in Spain. While you could check with your service provider about coverage before you leave, using your own service in roaming mode will involve additional costs. The alternative is to purchase a Spanish SIM card to use during your stay in Spain.

Spain has four mobile networks. They are Movistar, Vodafone, Orange and Yoiga. Buying a Spanish SIM card is relatively simple and inexpensive. By law, you will be required to show some form of identification such as a passport. A basic SIM card from Vodafone costs €5. There are two tourist packages available for €15, which offers a combination of 1Gb data, together with local and international call time. Alternately, a data only package can also be bought for €15. From Orange, you can get a SIM card for free, with a minimum top-up purchase of €10. A tourist SIM with a combination of data and voice calls can be bought for €15. Movistar offers a start-up deal of €10. At their sub-branches, Tuenti, you can also get a free SIM, but the catch is that you need to choose a package to get it. The start-up cost at Yoiga is €20.

🌐 Dialling Code

The international dialling code for Spain is +34.

GRANADA TRAVEL GUIDE

🌐 Emergency Numbers

All Emergencies: 112 (no area code required)

Police (municipal): 092

Police (national): 091

Police (tourist police, Madrid): 91 548 85 37

Police (tourist police, Barcelona): 93 290 33 27

Ambulance: 061 or 112

Fire: 080 or 112

Traffic: 900 123 505

Electricity: 900 248 248

Immigration: 900 150 000

MasterCard: 900 958 973

Visa: 900 99 1124

🌐 Public Holidays

1 January: New Year's Day (Año Nuevo)

6 January: Day of the Epiphany/Three Kings Day (Reyes Mago)

March/April: Good Friday

1 May: Labor Day (Día del Trabajo)

15 August: Assumption of Mary (Asunción de la Virgen)

12 October: National Day of Spain/Columbus Day (Fiesta Nacional de España or Día de la Hispanidad)

GRANADA TRAVEL GUIDE

1 November: All Saints Day (Fiesta de Todos los Santos)

6 December: Spanish Constitution Day (Día de la Constitución)

8 December: Immaculate Conception (La Immaculada)

25 December: Christmas (Navidad)

Easter Monday is celebrated in the Basque region, Castile-La Mancha, Catalonia, La Rioja, Navarra and Valencia. 26 December is celebrated as Saint Stephen's Day in Catalonia and the Balearic Islands.

🌎 Time Zone

Spain falls in the Central European Time Zone. This can be calculated as Greenwich Mean Time/Co-ordinated Universal Time (GMT/UTC) +2; Eastern Standard Time (North America) -6; Pacific Standard Time (North America) -9.

🌎 Daylight Savings Time

Clocks are set forward one hour on the last Sunday in March and set back one hour on the last Sunday in October for Daylight Savings Time.

GRANADA TRAVEL GUIDE

🌎 School Holidays

Spain's academic year is from mid-September to mid-June. It is divided into three terms with two short breaks of about two weeks around Christmas and Easter.

🌎 Trading Hours

Trading hours in Spain usually run from 9.30am to 1.30pm and from 4.30pm to 8pm, from Mondays to Saturdays. Malls and shopping centers often trade from 10am to 9pm without closing. During the peak holiday seasons, shops could stay open until 10pm. Lunch is usually served between 1pm and 3.30pm while dinner is served from 8.30 to 11pm.

🌎 Driving Laws

The Spanish drive on the right hand side of the road. You will need a driver's licence which is valid in the EC to be able to hire a car in Spain. The legal driving age is 18, but most rental companies will require you to be at least 21 to be able to rent a car. You will need to carry your insurance documentation and rental contract with you at all times, when driving. The speed limit in Spain is 120km per hour on motorways, 100km per hour on dual carriageways and 90km per hour on single carriageways. Bear in mind that it is illegal to drive in Spain wearing sandals or flip-flops.

You may drive a non-Spanish vehicle in Spain provided that it is considered roadworthy in the country where it is registered. As a UK resident, you will be able to drive a vehicle registered in the UK in Spain for up to six months, provided that your liabilities as a UK motorist, such as MOT, road tax and insurance are up to date for the entire period of your stay. The legal limit in Spain is 0.05, but for new drivers who have had their licence for less than two years, it is 0.03.

🌐 Drinking Laws

In Spain, the minimum drinking age is 18. Drinking in public places is forbidden and can be punished with a spot fine. In areas where binge drinking can be a problem, alcohol trading hours are often limited.

🌐 Smoking Laws

In the beginning of 2006, Spain implemented a policy banning smoking from all public and private work places. This includes schools, libraries, museums, stadiums, hospitals, cinemas, theatres and shopping centers as well as public transport. From 2011, smoking was also banned in restaurants and bars, although designated smoking areas can be created provided they are enclosed and well ventilated. Additionally tobacco products may only be sold from tobacconists and bars and restaurants where smoking is permitted. Smoking near children's parks, schools or health centers carries a €600 fine.

🌎 Electricity

Electricity: 220 volts

Frequency: 50 Hz

Your electrical appliances from the UK and Ireland should be able to function sufficiently in Spain, but since Spain uses 2 pin sockets, you will need a C/F adapter to convert the plug from 3 to 2-pins. The voltage and frequency is compatible with UK appliances. If travelling from the USA, you will need a converter or step-down transformer to convert your appliances to 110 volts. The latest models of many laptops, camcorders, cell phones and digital cameras are dual-voltage with a built in converter.

🌎 Food & Drink

Spanish cuisine is heavily influenced by a Moorish past. Staple dishes include the rice dish, Paella, Jamon Serrano (or Spanish ham), Gazpacho (cold tomato-based vegetable soup), roast suckling pig, chorizo (spicy sausage) and the Spanish omelette. Tapas (hot or cold snacks) are served with drinks in Spanish bars.

The most quintessentially Spanish drink is sangria, but a popular alternative with the locals is tinto de verano, or summer wine, a mix of red wine and lemonade. Vino Tinto or red wine compliments most meal choices. The preferred red grape type is Tempranillo, for which the regions of Roija and Ribera del Duero are famous. A well-known sparkling wine, Cava, is grown in Catalonia. Do try the Rebujito, a Seville style mix of sherry, sparkling water and mint. The most popular local beers are Cruzcampo, Alhambra and Estrello Damm. Coffee is also popular with Spaniards, who prefer Café con leche (espresso with milk).

Websites

http://www.idealspain.com

A detailed resource that includes legal information for anyone planning a longer stay or residency in Spain.

http://spainattractions.es/

http://www.tourspain.org/

http://spainguides.com/

http://www.travelinginspain.com/

http://wikitravel.org/en/Spain

GRANADA TRAVEL GUIDE

Printed in Great Britain
by Amazon